The Singer's Broken Throat

The Singer's Broken Throat

Including The Trinity Poems

Des Walsh

TALONBOOKS
2003

Talonbooks
P.O. Box 2076, Vancouver, British Columbia, Canada V6B 3S3
www.talonbooks.com

Typeset in Garamond and printed and bound in Canada.

First Printing: October 2003

A few of these poems have previously appeared in the anthologies, *Tickle Ace* and *The Backyards of Heaven*.

National Library of Canada Cataloguing in Publication Data

Walsh, Des
  The singer's broken throat / Des Walsh.

Poems.
ISBN 0-88922-478-1

I. Title.
PS8595.A586S56 2003   C811'.54   C2003-910962-3

The publisher gratefully acknowledges the financial support of the Canada Council for the Arts; the Government of Canada through the Book Publishing Industry Development Program; and the Province of British Columbia through the British Columbia Arts Council for our publishing activities.

for Ruth

Glynmill Inn Bar, Corner Brook, December 4, 1992

The purple raven has no compassion
for the wooden parrot,
whose fixed decorative gaze doesn't move,
more like a verdict than a sentence.
The raven, however, blinks like a
Christmas bulb, its heart flutters
like a carol, no more or less than the
paganism of Christian sacrifice.
And like the raven,
we look to the green bough
to protect us from the falling
frequent snow, to nest in the
holy, holly, holiday,
and kiss each others' frozen smiles.

New World Island, Notre Dame Bay

He was in Moreton's Harbour
going out of tune caressing
the lichen-covered myths.
The lump on his head
seemed to be larger now,
settling neatly on the hairline
just above his loneliness.
She got excited
and whispered how much
more of him there was to know
and that in the morning
she enjoyed his poetry
more than fresh-squeezed orange juice.
Ah the world is good he sighed
as he whistled his way around the circle
and doffed his cap to those who cared.

Mornings mourning

(a sonnet for CBC Morningside, aired May 13, 1993)

This morning in a cove in Newfoundland
light winds have become increasingly strong
not because of a cry, nor even commands
do we raise our fists to what has gone wrong.
A nation of people fall to their knees
bowing to Canada's years of abuse
my people kiss the anxiety of trees
too dignified to fight the foreign ruse.
Mornings here are too politically sour
when families in harbours look to sea
where this morning's sun begins to cower
and kitchen voices mumble can it be.
    No fish, no mornings that they understand
    God guard thee, God guard thee, dear Newfoundland.

Vous êtes Acadie, je suis Terre Neuve

Never had the landscape of Cape Breton
been so unpredictable, foreigners both,
the American car carried us across
centuries of meadows and
pools of singing, our voices penetrating
the dashboard, seeping through
the molded metal to find their way
to a dandelion's heart, its embrace as
fragile as literature, its future as
secure as a mother's breast.
I was weeping when Jesus was crucified,
I was weeping when your people
were driven from the coast,
just as I am weeping now,
when I rise above the meadow
and look down on a man in love,
throwing stones into Bras D'or Lake,
knowing his life has changed forever
and every seagull's cry will be his own.
I know now that they will name
a constellation after us, and no lovers
will look at the night sky without shading
their eyes and breaking into song.
They will count their lucky stars,
just as I have counted every second
since I last saw you, when even my own people
gave no comfort, and the smell of the sea
only meant distance and that tonight,
you lie somewhere in Canada,
with the moisture of your mouth
still soothing the side of my face
that has burned relentlessly
since I fell to my knees
and told God I will love you forever.

Talamh an Éisc (Land of the Fish)

for Paddy Keenan

Across an ocean of salt-drenched myths
this is where we live now
this is where we belong,
our hearts lined with fragments,
and like the lichen-covered rock
unaffected by storm.
Our souls are in every boulder
that inches its way to the sea,
we rule the meadows they
have claimed and the
gulls that rest there.
We sing to the drowned
tear-soaked families and
cling to the broken truths that
made us call this home, our voices
crying out over the pounding waves
only to be blown back to a sparrow's throat,
to have the melody cradled
in the arms of spruce and wind.
We are the songs of weather.
Back then, when these harbours
showed themselves only to
St. Brendan and the Beothuck
we came for fish, their scales becoming ours,
their justice becoming ours.
Back then, when the echoes of a
single note would ring out and
caress our granite graves
we would sing ourselves from sleep,
women would kiss the ocean,
their mouths smoothing the water that has
called us all back, to this place,
to hear that note again, which
will sound in our hearts forever.

Saturday, September 4, 2:46 AM, 1993

This is not to say
birds aren't singing
in some love-worn meadow
or that planets aren't blinking
for those that want to see them.
This is not to say
rain isn't smoothing
some sun-drenched heart
or that liquor isn't soothing
the singer's broken throat.
This is nothing more
than what it is,
a man home,
where the cry
of a brittle leaf
is as loud as the battle
any soldier has heard …
good night sweet dancer,
a poet turns his eyes to you.

Poem for the Peter Gzwoski Golf Invitational, Bally Haly, September 25, 1992

(sponsored by Petro Canada to the tune of $200.00, but as of this date, August 4, 2003, the poet has not been paid his fee)

It's 8:00 AM, Friday, September 25,
we're in a holding pattern, a frost delay.
I study the photographs in the clubhouse,
circa 1907, sheep on the fairways
looking more rested than the poet.

8:30 AM, we start on the fourteenth tee
where Jed Long gives me my first beer.
What was once the property of the
Job's, the Harvey's and the Crosbie's
has now become the poet's arena.

I'm looking around to see who's here …
Deputy Mayor Andy Wells looking for stray golfers,
hoping he finds them before
city council puts them down.

Len Simms is opposing his teammates club selection …
I study the unconstitutional swing of the Premier.

Back to the game, we're not in good shape,
our club pro just put one twenty feet in front of the tee.
He makes fun of the Petro Canada Poet Laureate,
the fabrication of fossil fuels.

My brain wanders, I think of Wayne Rostad and Murray McLaughlin,
the fact they were given bottles of Newfoundland's Newman's Port …
Christ … Canadians, since 1949
we've given them the best of everything.

16th hole … poet makes a putt.

A CBC camera crew inches their way across a fairway,
there's an urgent message for Premier Wells,
they want his reaction ... seems Joey Smallwood and
Elvis have been found living together in Buchan's Junction.

Back to the game ... oh no, number 17!
My worst goddamn hole
a poet's nightmare, it's like
walking into the misguided life of a publisher.

We're moving fast, we come upon Bruce's ducks,
he calls them birdies, but I know they're ducks.
The cool light of angels fall,
our putts don't.

Yet, as we approach our final hole,
I think again of the munching sheep
and how a certain CBC journalist scolded us ...
to him I raise my illiterate 3 iron
until I hear him bleat,
late into the loon-filled night.

Jesus … our knees are raw from praying

I believe in these angels
that caress my neck,
their lonely journey
pressed against my memory of God
and my spinner-yielding youth.
These days are full of that past,
when sun-drenched, pale wood
moved with water and ice.
I remember that one glimmering fish
from Neville's wharf in Jersey Side,
that one scream from a soft voice
I still hear, singing through
the language of fish and the running
torment that make a country.
    There's a fish and a soft voice in Belleoram
    the world must see and hear …
    like angels, their hearts beat faster than the pulse of Tokyo
    with all the passion of drowning sailors,
    whose own hearts were crushed by a maple leaf
    and torn by the thorns that now cut their children.

On a train heading west of Sussex, along the St. John River, April 11, 1994

Each tree
an island in
a swollen
river.
A sanctuary
for orphaned ice.

On a train heading east of St. Hyacinthe, Quebec,
April 18, 1994

This pale moon reflects only
those winged images I allow myself.
The cup-rattling dining car moves east
but not home. This is not home.
My moon kisses the faces of Burgeo
and reminds them of tides and desire
while I sing to broken trees and ask every woman
to be lenient. I sing to you on Elgin Street and pray
my voice touches the seaweed tears where I live, where
I hold my family like broken glass, every piece necessary,
every roll of the wheel home necessary.

But somewhere tonight in the Arabian sky,
a joyous moon wraps itself in sensuality
and shines on us forever.

On a train heading east of Sherbrooke, Quebec,
April 18, 1994

So now he will go in front of the world
and tell the truth. You are more beautiful
than flowers think themselves, your petals
far more fragrant, your eyes far more damaging.
The twisted, flaccid stems of the world bow to you,
their only purpose to show what happens
when you ignore them. God knows this, as do I, it's
our only reason for waiting. And this poem, we hold
to our breasts and think of you.

The Rhythm of Windows

Last night, there was only one light from your house,
maybe the child was sleeping, his fears surrendering to
the bright comfort and your eyes, forever on his perfect face.
Outside, I sang to both of you, my alcohol eyes as
wet as whiskey. I sang for a thousand years, and
while the wars raged, not even the enemies of love
would dare arrest the song or the singer,
leaving them both for the curious and
the nocturnal, letting daybreak do its damage
to all champions of the heart that meet on the
corner of Gower and Cathedral St., where only the
bravest wait patiently for the end of the world.

Those New World Island berries
are for the sweetest of tongues
(for Larry Small, June 6, 1994)

The road to Tizzard's Harbour is longer
than most people think. No map shows us
the distance from your back-porch landing
to the crest of Jack Snap, but I feel every step
when you raise your voice above the shallow
graves of Moreton's Harbour men. I know that
fifty-three years ago there was an understanding
between you and the berry-picking ghosts of "Sligo shore,"
where faces cut from centuries of too much pain contort
with the memory of their own silken beauty,
how they would press themselves into those they loved
and cry out for you as you do them, when the last fish
throws itself into the burning horizon and the sea
is no longer there for your father to walk on.

Oh Jesus, guide this light

Oh Jesus, guide this light,
let it touch the Northern Peninsula
and shower travellers with the warmth of stories.
Back here, our cold footprints are avoided
by the most careful of fall birds. Back here,
stories of heroes are making headlines ...
the poets are touching themselves again,
the fallen leaves are swirling.
There is no ceremony now,
only the sound of tires on a wet street,
the songs from a couch creep into a dog's ears.
The singer is restless, he dials again, the same message,
yet that voice alone can make every lover lonely.
Every lover of the broken song
is calling to you ... don't leave us,
our windows are open
and the song is perfect,
protects the burning flower.

On being Catholic and loving the treachery of winter

November winds move these leaves toward
insensible geographical landmarks where
people kneel and pray to be found.
Patrick Street is like that, the worthy and
the truthful have all lived there,
their voices singing over church spires,
both their tongues speaking to their own God.
I park my car next to what was always William's Grocery,
about twelve doors down and east of what was then the
Newfoundland Nail and Foundry, where galvanized
receptacles measured out a life's work in inches and pounds of metal.
I'll always stop and look at the tree where
he fell and died, frightened I'm told,
by the Wesley United Church Minister,
scolded for stealing chestnuts from the welcoming tree on
sacred property. And suddenly I'm reminded again that
down the street, St. Patrick's Church entertained no natural growth,
being housed only in stone, and that my love for you is its only salvation,
when snow crusts itself to the burning bark and God lets me touch you again.

The pipes crack and footsteps are still heard

The pipes crack and footsteps are still heard
from another time, the resounding patter of children.
This, in the middle of my longing, is a perfect time,
all my truths abandoned, all my appetite hovering.
Has God ever reached out and placed his perfect lips
on the back of your hand ... he has mine.
It's become swollen from kissing it, sometimes
I've actually let my teeth bite the sacred flesh,
heard choirs of the lonely call out to me
themselves full of love and hunger.
If I could protect myself from you, from God,
I would swim over the broken lives and
put my mouth on your breasts forever, my tongue
never flaccid, would mold itself into syllables
and find a place to settle on your happy, new lips.
In the kitchen, I am pressing my warm cheek
to the cool canvas floor. This is how I want you now,
this is how I think the world should be.

I see horses at the edge of the earth

I see horses at the edge of the earth
as lonely as any weeping landwash,
as lonely as any prayer.
This is my worst moment,
all boundaries of fences and light
have decayed or feverishly diminished,
I can't see you. Nothing will sleep, nothing will stop,
I'm the only one to feed this burning heart.
If I were to fall from moist cliffs
people would whisper that I'd kissed
the lips of a song and cradled its fragrant curse.
Others would shout, he'd opened his arms too often,
the hazards of living on an island ... alone.

Thoughts on the health of those we love

Now I know the suffering
of burning embers,
their last breath sighs
over broken beaches,
their burning hearts
smolder in the sensual
curve of dreams.
You looked so perfect
for a sick woman, your face
shining out onto the street
of legends, St. Patrick himself
questioning your health.
In a biblical sense,
your voice crashed against
the purest breast, your waving
signal beat nations of
soldiers into submission ...
but here, among the misspelled lives
of misplaced sailors, we care little
for foreign wars, our own battles
more hazardous than the promise of fortune.

Hotel Inter-Continental, Room 311, Toronto, April 18, 1995
(for Jonathan Butler on his birthday)

Oh Newfoundland, have I got to leave you
to seek employment in a foreign land,
forced from my nation from cruel taxation
I now must leave you dear Newfoundland
　　　　　　　—traditional

From your house to Brunswick and Bloor
you turn right, I think that's east.
East is home, past pounds of concrete and steel,
past generations who think themselves from the coast
to the real home of heroes, where
one hundred miles of ocean
separates Canada from perfect language.

A voice called to me from Yonge and Wellesley,
squat and almost lifeless …
I thought of your mother's people
how they would lean closer and protect her,
how every Newfoundlander would cry for someone
who has never known the word home.
How a sudden scream of sirens and voices
reminds all from there that where we're from
is a gift, something we open at birth
and carry with us for the rest of our lives.

I have missed so much, known so many melodies

If ever the word lonely
were to be etched on a man's heart
it would be mine.
I've counted every gust of wind,
every syllable of the best-loved songs,
every mystery since time began
only to be here again, alone.
There's no comfort in knowing
that you, a cure for this,
are asleep on the highway
with nothing more than memory
and every fallen mythology.
The Iroquois, who are known
to acknowledge the sanctity of female power,
would not have martyred you
as the Huns did St. Ursula.
They'd be more like me,
wait until you signal
before coming to your feet
and ask nothing more
than to be with you.

How love endures after the third day

His voice startled me.
I wanted it to be yours
caressing me with syllables
manipulating the flow of blood
as it always does, stirring the loose
debris from the corners
of my heart as it always does.
He told me you were sleeping
and I knew he could see you
your hair across the pillow
your tongue gently moistening
the dryness on your lips.
I know your fingers
are coloured by the dye of fabric
and stiff from the monotony
of needle and threat.
But no matter what he says
his costume doesn't fit you.
Mine however, its tattered edges
brushing against your breasts
will be with you always.
One other thing …
I know you feel this poem now
and you stir slightly because of it.
At least I have that.

Pius Power Jr., Caul's Funeral Home, June 1, 1996

My friend, a former United Church minister,
acknowledging the crosses on Caul's doors,
remarked that the Catholics get you
even before entering. Fair play I thought.
My first time seeing those crosses was 1968.
My mother, cold from hours of death,
surrendered and fell into character.
Not you Pius. Your eyes opened and
fell on mine, your too-often neglected
journey blinded me, me aware of my
place here, set against yours and
your father's before you. Your eyes, wide and awake,
were singing "Mowing Meadows Down," and I, like
the fool I am, thought I knew the words.
And when I heard the story of earlier,
how they had to glue your hands together to keep
them resting in the ordered way I thought,
good thing you're only singing in my heart,
for if you were to sit up and break into it,
your hands would swing, and Newfoundland,
knowing its loss, would hold them forever.

A Sunday in October

There's a certain slant of light on winter afternoons
that oppresses like the weight of cathedral tunes
                          —Emily Dickinson

It may only be fall
but this light is no less damaging.
The heaviness of blood is self-evident
the struggle for fluid movement
when one foot refuses to obey the other.
I have watched armies of birds gather
in nearby trees and along phone lines,
themselves full of anticipation, ignoring
the screams of those below them,
content with the distance.
Unlike those birds, I am never
content with distance. My wings,
forever flapping, hovering somewhere
near you and your father's picture,
are perfectly rhythmic on this
October day, when leaves are scattering
and stray dogs wander relentlessly
in search of food and a place to piss …
happy hunting to all of us, I say.

On hearing the question answered

So now it's come to this,
the crucifying threat.
"I can't say it won't happen."
A line similar to Judas,
a line the world continues to suffer from.
When you lie next to him
I'll be in a crowded room
reading about your beauty
stabbing the air with syllables
nervously tapping my breast
while each nail is expertly driven
and the miners of poetry
gasp at the trickles of blood.
Each in their own way will hate
what you have done, wanting nothing more
than to kiss my pierced side
and swallow the pungent life
never to sing your praises again.
The singer's throat is slit.

If I should stain the earth with tears

If I should stain the earth with tears
would you linger long enough to collect them,
petal-like, sweetened by the stems of grasses.
The moistened meadows corrupted by anxious
wails from dream-laden birds are only there
for you, sweet protector. And your mysterious arms,
themselves full of anyone they wish to embrace.
I call to you from my stubbornness, from my crown
of guilt and passion. I call to you for forgiveness
for all the sleeplessness I have given you. I call to you
for a fair trial. Let me stand once more and look into
your perfect heart and feel my parched mouth
against the grain of your commitment. If then
you need to turn away, I will find the scorched
hand of the devil, and weep I will, my tears
never again to touch your burning landscape.

Oh Canada

the bilingual translators for the executioners
the chauffeurs of North American whiskey
—Pablo Neruda

I have seen the damage
from Trepassey to Plum Point,
the beached bones of nationhood
corroded like dreams of plenty.
This is not part of my memory,
of fish and gardens, of boiled singing mackerel
and steaming plates of enough, for us
and the bold barking dogs.
The rust-teary eyes of pride
fall away into unkempt weed-happy meadows
where no animals move under the weight
of the moon, no lovers under
the weight of each other. Look at us now
Oh Canada. We are indeed the songs
of weather, bleating across the Gulf,
no sheep-shorn melodies left, little dignity
left to die for, no spires to erect.

I have seen the damage of fifty years on the rotting planks
of skiffs, their stem heads arching to God
their keels buried in the lifeless landwash
while U-Hauls convoy west, passed Pearson's Peak
to seed the factories and kitchens
and soup lines of North America.

I have seen the damage and I hate you for it.
I hate your maple leaf and your anthem.
And for those who accuse me,
those of us who are left with the truth
say to you with honour and passion,
damn you and your thievery,

damn you and your cold, calculating colonialism.
And while guarding what's left
of our pine clad hills,
we bend over and moon the Gulf, Oh Canada,
and ask you to kiss our collective arse.

March 3, 1999—Notes on an upcoming anniversary

We are North Americans now
the same as those Pablo Neruda wearied of,
lulled into the same crimes,
the same culture-starved wanderings.
Fifty years ago we were Europeans,
singing stubbornly into the face of wind
cutting masts for schooners that would sail forever,
cutting pine for the churches of England.
Fifty years ago we were lean and sensual,
our mouths unhurriedly pressed into each other,
our tongues touched whatever God we wanted.
Before our glistening fish, salted for Portugal
and Spain, became the currency of theatre,
before being slaughtered in wars far from
the coves we wandered as children,
we pressed wild berries to our lips
and wiped the pungent juices from our mouths,
the blood red placenta of the promise of a healthy future.
And now, the disease spreading, we weep together,
collectively walking to every graveyard on every headland
and bury men and rodneys, women and knowledge.
We close the lodges and the halls, remove the steeples,
abandon the headstones, haul the doors of the trap, leave rosary beads
between stone and seaweed, leave saw blades to rust behind hills,
half-empty dippers of berries spilling into the mossy barrens, leave
our sensuality circling the tops of fog-wrapped fir trees.
And now, fifty years later, having done as we're told,
we are left to celebrate.

I love you more than any God, not falsely

I love you more than any God, not falsely,
for reasons that would dim the brightest star
Your family knows this, they see it when
I genuflect as you pass. It isn't simply
how your hair falls across your eyes
or how your laughter subdues
the most anxious of moments
or even how your breasts lay beneath me,
it's the simple purity of love.
I know St. Jacques and the history
of where you're from, it's a French name.
Perhaps that's why foreigners circle you
like half-starved crows, thinking their
accents are enough to impress
the most wandering flower.
My family has a history as well,
we watch you everywhere.
Did you know there are Walsh's in Fleur de Lys?

Tonight

Tonight, the poet eats lamb and zucchini,
a few small potatoes the French go on so much about
and some steamed green beans,
enough to satisfy the hungriest of lonely people.
But knowing the e-string is broken on his fiddle
cripples him in a way that disturbs him,
he has no source of wailing
no way to reach out to his sad misfortune.
If he opens the blind onto Gower St.
he sees nothing but the lost and broken hearted,
the remnants of another poem,
those he has held as close to his heart as fishermen.
Checking for beeps on his answering service
he waits like Joan of Arc, his burning unequaled,
his path already chosen, as passionate as Christ.

I have no other way of saying this ...
if you hurt me, I'll kill you.

I think of you always

I think of you always,
sometimes under the sway
of baring maples and oaks,
the cool November winds
numbing their branches.
A lone sparrow cuts a path.

I am like a meandering neighbourhood dog
out for comfort, the relentless search
for anything while acknowledging the
Sunday afternoon loneliness
of a crow in a public park.
A child falls from a swing and cries.

Please let me know you think of me
any sign would calm things, ease
my desire to abandon comfort and end my days
in Tierra Del Fuego, lost in the burning sun of missionaries
never to touch your mouth again.
A plane engine roars.

My heart is as big as a field

My heart is as big as a field.
It bounces over rocks and collides with insects
You scatter as you pass.
We were here before,
When women and men laboured
To erect their perfect boundaries
And call the field their own.
Somehow now, when crows are all
That inch their way through my eyes
I still see you, naked and immaculate
Beneath the perfect agony of boughs.
My lips nowhere near you,
My arms tearing at the long grass
That all have ignored and forgotten.

But then, that's how you see me
Tongue-starved under the unforgiving spruce
Calling out to see you once more
Until the alarm sounds again,
And I place my hands on myself
And turn my wet mouth
Into the flower-ridden pillow.

Antibiotics

I have black Irish crows
in my chest
I cough them up
on the road to Corifin,
splattering the faded
lime-washed stone walls
with black feathers and whiskey.
The doctor in Ennis
who chose the Bahamas over Newfoundland
tells me the infection is genetic,
my people coming from Cork,
and that my cure is with the pills
and not to kiss the bare rock of the Burren
and ignore any shrine to the Blessed Virgin.
That said, I press my dry mouth
to the history of stone and
light candles and say three Hail Mary's
at every crossroad in Clare.
I may indeed swallow his medicine
but I'm no fool.

Ballyvaughan, County Clare, Ireland
October 2nd, 2000

On a train heading northeast
(from Cork to Dublin, October 18, 2000)

Outside the boundaries of ancient and formica
The rain-spattered train window
Allows me an image of cows, sheep and memory.
I leave Cork different than you, Thomas Walsh,
I move inland, my back to the harbour
While you, your eyes straining to see
Around the point in or about 1852,
Probably didn't suspect the shock
On turning your gaze back
To a disappearing headland,
Your last image of home.
What hills of these were yours I wonder
What myths did you carry with you
That now swirl inside me all these years later
When I too disappear into the arms of legend
Call the magpies by name and think of home,
Where sea foam tumbles over rocks and
Whispers to me that crows too have names
And every stone in Newfoundland has a reason
As perfect as the curved line of spruce
As perfect as all of us who come from that chosen ground.

This dust-covered life

This dust-covered life is so full
of the fingerprints of a man crawling,
this creased heart so full
of the clawmarks of a man wandering.
This anxiety-infected landscape,
where once, the sweet breath of angels
calmed all burning desire, calls out
in its raggedness to be re-mapped.
I call on you, with your wet cartographer's eyes ...
have a look at this, and if you see fit,
warn others not to come this way,
where only wings of burden
flutter erratically in front of nothing familiar,
yet somehow carve your name on the hills of St. Jacques
for only me to see ... forever.

When I think of you far away

When I think of you far away
it's like reading a novel
I never quite understand ...
too many characters,
too many twists and turns
that are never resolved.

I've never attempted a novel,
a short story once,
but too many words
too many lies.

And with that,
I condemn everyone
who thinks I'm crying ...

I once said that my heart was as big as a field

I once said that my heart was as big as a field.
It isn't ... it's more the size of a hole
that would receive a modest fence post,
one that would surely fall in on itself
and need repairing. Horses trod over me and
drop their belongings into my throat. I gag
on the taste of putrefied hay and the memory
of fresh acres of flowers. God bless the house
I say, but I'm not Irish ... I am more of the granite,
cold and lifeless like your heart, sinking forever
in the lifeless sea that was once home to our
people, but is now nothing but a drunken memory
that never goes away, that never caresses kelp
with the same sensuality, never sways back and forth
with the hope of someday being held and kept in one place.

October 29, 2001

Today, the sky here
is as blue as God
will allow it,
and the light as soft as
Fortune Bay when it
calms itself from torment.
Across this ocean
all things will calm themselves.
All seabirds will nest for you,
all banners will wave for you
when you return and your smiling face
is the only thing I see.
But for now, let the Irish enjoy themselves,
They deserve your beauty, as does every headland of home.

The sky is blue again today

The sky is blue again today
But I don't see it.
I see a dismal sky,
One I would easily dismiss
As a feeble sky, a useless sky.
Probably not like the sky over Inishbofin,
Which I'm sure is full of the sounds of
Life and your laughter, your songs
Timidly seducing all around you.
Oh yes, I know these things,
I've been to Inishbofin
And I know the damage it can do.

Do you know what you're doing?
I ask this as I call your
Answering machine just to hear your voice,
I wanted to leave a message saying
I hate the Irish, that I hate
What they've made us.
Two people separated by
An ocean and a simple fucking telephone call.

So I'm going to drink now
And curse that sky we share
And mark this day of November 4, 2001
As the day I left you to your selfishness,
Dún Gráinne, and the mythology of love.

This way

The lights of St. John's shimmer
Through the dancing branches.
It is a cold November night and the
Ashes from the day's fire are mute and cold.
I spoke with my mother again
She told me I was right to long
And whisper your name in the hallway
Its echo still vibrating in the dark staircase
That I've passed twenty-seven times today.
Between the railings is where I imagined
I saw your face, your mouth pressed against
The dark wood, your lips moistening the driest
Of long-ago life. I've removed my mouth from
That spot long enough to write this and
Leave this thought with you … I'll leave the door
Open and light the fire, no more of the lonely, my face
Will be as warm as hearts touching,
As warm as a path home.

John's Pond (Lake St. John)

It's Tuesday night on Middle Ridge,
eight miles east of John's Pond (Lake St. John on
the official map). My friends are hunting
the caribou, gone off like mummers in festive colours
earlier in the day, hoping for triumphant return
in the now black of night. My triumphant return
is to you, my feet wet from meandering
on damp bogs, praying that you still love me
while calling your name from Pinsent's Ridge
hoping you stir from whatever comfort finds you
and that you taste my lips while holding your breasts,
knowing there's a man alone in the woods
whose only longing is to press you
gently against the largest of spruce and show
grey jays what a melody really is.

The Trinity Poems

The triangle of the heart
(for Thomas Walsh 1847–1952)

I will monitor the movement of tides
and wait anxiously for the shipping news
out of Trinity, where men mumble
among themselves and talk fairies and Greek legend.
It is said that Fahey's Point touches
the salt thighs of angels and that there,
my great-grandfather from Cork turned
his eyes to Ireland and wept for you,
one hundred and thirty-two years before you
ran your fingers along lime-washed picket fences
and bent slowly to kiss a stone. I am with him now.
We both walk the lanes of that place and watch
for any sign of you, each of us startled by the rush of
wings and the sensuous lapping of the ocean's cool, wet mouth.

Trinity Pageant, Trinity, Newfoundland

On Fleet Street in Trinity
the sign reads 1830 ...
a time when the lust of angels
was as passionate as rain
and the pageantry of fish
fell dutifully from the moist lips of choirs.
Here now, I fit comfortably in period clothes,
my tear-streaked face blending well with weather,
my heart pounding for the mouth of Mary Moores,
my tongue tracing her carved granite marker
while the eyes of Trinity follow the poet
his love for her more overwhelming than history
his desire as perfect as a partridgeberry.

On a bus heading east,
near North Sydney, Cape Breton

Each small brook, I hear them babbling.
I hear their whispering, pebble-littered voices
calling me across one hundred miles of water ...
itself, salt-perfect and lascivious,
knowing my obsession in feeling it
below my broken life.
One hundred miles of open sea,
five hundred and twenty-eight thousand feet
before I touch the same ground you walk on.
Listen for it, I will pound the rocks in Port aux Basques
to let you know I'm home and then,
if you bend to kiss a Trinity stone
your mouth will give life
to all who sing their way back to you
along Newfoundland's melody-filled roads.

When singers gather, they will look to me for forgiveness when they raise their voices and sing of the damage your eyes have done

This is my story ...
little souvenirs of you
still cling to my breast
as I look to the sky to
determine the weather in Trinity.
A blown canvas sail wraps me in desire,
my thighs wet with salt-water rhythm.
Newfoundland, my country,
sings to me in these days of wonder,
but always, your voice calls out
over the cries of seabirds.
Do I go down to the water now ...

Here, with the memory of your burning tongue
across my breast, I am as lonely as any shipwreck,
my song kisses every stone across this meandering landwash,
the souls of those before me wail at the perverted sea.

I've taught myself a lot today

I've taught myself a lot today.
Like how to imagine the moon in my arms
and you ignoring it as you should.
I've taught myself that a ticking clock is death,
my only way of telling the truth.

I want you to sleep now as I write this.
I want you to hate me, hate my desire.
Hate how I've broken the rose
and left the notes of a song colliding on Fahey's Neck,
each one fragrantly different, each one imperfect.

I've taught myself other things.
Like how reassuring death can be
and that finally, when all is equal
and the earth's tongue slips between your own lips,
you'll cry out for me in a way even I'll believe.

Wednesday

We watched it for ten days,
one lone trap-boat, its patterned rhythm
echoing off our hearts as it made its way
across the water and out through Trinity Harbour.
Each morning we followed its wake
and waited anxiously for evening's return ...
the sound first, then the stem-head rounding the point.

It's almost light now, the lone hand is at the tiller and soon,
he will pass Hog's Nose and probably look up.
He will notice the empty window, no figures standing,
he will sense the emptiness of the house, once music-filled,
and know we're far away from the Trinity light
and sensing you without me,
know this has been the longest night of my life ...
he will never pass that way without wishing the world felt the same,
wishing our embraces still disturbed Trinity doves
and we could watch him forever,
our lips smoothing the strongest of winds.

We sing like any other broken path

Don't shake the rainbows from your hair,
too many of us depend on it.
We realign moonbeams to be close to you,
anything to confuse those who want your sweetness.
Back here, the roads walked are naked,
their meandering songs collide with nothing but truth
as dancers stumble through New Bonaventure, their arms
reaching for anyone to hold, their hearts calling for wind.
Is it true, that when you sleep away from home,
angels reschedule their shifts to be close to you, and
Jesus, and those closest to him, stir uncomfortably ...
In Trinity, the headstone of Mary Moores is said to call out,
and even those resettled from Ireland's Eye,
are known to be without purpose since you've left us.

Come back to the melody
sweet wanderer of islands and revolutions,
a nation of lovers calls to you.

Black Bird

If I stand long enough under the spires
of churches, if I stay long enough
to see you through the colour
of your scarred window, I'll see you
kiss the dried, broken rose.
Out here, my guardian angel and I hover
at the edge of language, both our tongues
slide over the edge of winter ...
glass tears collect on our wings.

Yesterday, coming back to you,
Trinity was sun-bleached,
its reflection bounced off the moons
of Jupiter and shone back on your deceptive mouth.
I know this by the way crows shielded their eyes
from you and wept, as only crows can do, their
screaming disturbing the safest embrace.

The Launch, Trinity Shipbuilders, Trinity, June 24, 1995

I was with men, women and children
who through their tears have
launched boats for generations,
whose fathers and mothers suffered
through seasons of "low water, Sundays
and a ticking clock." We launched
that boat (a membrane of new wood and
old history) in a harbour where my
great-grandfather would have
whistled his way over The Dock,
passed Green's Garden, and shielded
his life from the glimmering,
death-ridden sea. The boat in the cradle,
we wove along the fence-lined roads of Trinity
in a festive carnival toward the landwash.
My friend, Rocky Henry Pearce Johnson
was at the wheel, my heart was at the wheel.
Children peddled alongside in full participation,
for this was their boat too. Curtains were pulled open,
older women, their arms folded in salute
smiled alongside their fragile older men,
all of us were in love for that perfect moment,
all of us were home.

Hog's Nose, Trinity

Your house has two eyes, both shut.
From here on Hog's Nose
I've tried to will them open,
have them see me from this side
walking blindly on the dark Nuddick
the slap slap of water calling below.
From Tavernor's Point they are less obvious
but still, like an oval-framed picture
of dead family, I sense them following me,
waiting for the decision ... I imagine them
springing open at the first sounds of struggle.
The first sounds of a drowning poet
doing as you wish and swimming to God's Cove
his seaweed heart pounding in white foam
crashing against the soon to be blood-stained rocks
that made us call this a good place to live.

Easter Weekend, April 22, 2001, Hog's Nose, Trinity

Ice in the harbour, like a single cawing crow,
Can be the loneliest sound. The last whisper
Surrounded by doubt and seduction, the grinding
Of pan against pan. Early spring is doubtful now,
The snow still crushing ole' Bill's ground and
Fahey's Neck colder than the bones of great-grandparents.
But then again, this is how it goes, the slow tedium of waiting
For the first glimmer of life, tinged with the first hint
Of a welcoming end. If ever Jesus came to the Bight
He would be welcome at this window, I would show him
Every fissure from Skerwink to Calf's Nose,
Every haunted moment from the Nuddick to Hog's Nose,
Every broken life that passes my view on the world
And calmly say, "Look ... do you see what you have done."
Then knowing from experience, would surely hear him say,
"God damn it all man, simply look the other way!"

And that said, God bless you all.

My eyes

There are too many men,
Too many eyes
Too many arms
You may want to hold ...
That surely want to hold you.

My comfort, however,
On this immaculate, star-filled night,
When Trinity Harbour hisses in its stillness
Is that I'm the only man still inside you ... I think?

I'm sorry, are you up
Are those my eyes you have open?

My friend's death
(for Al Pittman, 1940-2001)

I can tell you, now that you're dead,
I'm sick too Al, my heart heavier than
all the flowers of Russia. I used to think
that I would live forever ... I knew you
wouldn't, your eyes sunken from
the weight of lupins. I wanted to talk to you
about my illness, how the sadness sweeps
over me like broken glass, a small crack
and there it is ... all has to be replaced.
But what now? The lupins by the chapel
in Trinity are bulldozed into the earth
just a week before you were sentenced,
the last ones harvested were those you
picked for Alfreda, when you stooped as you
stumbled in the road, and your music-filled
heart allowed you to bouquet your way
to Rocky's Place for another performance and another
poem. Are you closer to the moon now, can you
reach out and wrap lilacs around it? I hope so ...
I can't, I'm sick ... my heart heavier than all the
flowers of Russia, all the flowers of St. Leonard's,
that will never bloom again, now that you've
resettled and left them and they've no reason
to cry out and call your name.